Cook Memorial Public Library

3 1122 01533 5354

MAR 2 6 2019

W9-AAT-547

MAR 2 6 2019

Make a Masterpiece

Charcoal

by Alix Wood

COOK MEMORIAL LIBRARY DISTRICT
413 N. MILWAUKEE AVE.
LIBERTYVILLE, ILLINOIS 60048

Gareth Stevens
PUBLISHING

Please visit our website, www.garethstevens.com. For a free color catalog of all our high-quality books, call toll free 1-800-542-2595 or fax 1-877-542-2596

Cataloging-in-Publication Data

Names: Wood, Alix.
Title: Charcoal / Alix Wood.
Description: New York : Gareth Stevens Publishing, 2019. | Series: Make a masterpiece | Includes glossary and index.
Identifiers: ISBN 9781538235836 (pbk.) | ISBN 9781538235959 (library bound) | ISBN 9781538235874 (6pack)
Subjects: LCSH: Charcoal drawing--Technique--Juvenile literature.
Classification: LCC NC850.W66 2019 | DDC 741.2'2--dc23

First Edition

Published in 2019 by
Gareth Stevens Publishing
111 East 14th Street, Suite 349
New York, NY 10003

© Alix Wood Books

Produced for Gareth Stevens by Alix Wood Books
Designed by Alix Wood
Editor: Eloise Macgregor

Photo credits:
Cover and title page background, 3 background, 10 bottom © Adobe Stock Images; 4, 10 background © public domain; all other images © Alix Wood

All rights reserved. No part of this book may be reproduced in any form without permission from the publisher, except by reviewer.

Printed in the United States of America

CPSIA compliance information: Batch #CW19GS For further information contact Gareth Stevens, New York, New York at 1-800-542-2595.

Contents

What Is Charcoal?

Charcoal is a black, crumbly drawing material made by burning sticks or **vines** in a **kiln** without air. Artists often use it for **sketching**, but it can be used to create finished drawings, too. Charcoal smudges easily, so it is not ideal for very detailed drawing. It is great for creating flowing sketches, or for dark, spooky pictures. If you learn to work with its smudginess, charcoal can help you make some really great art.

Charcoal was used to create some of the earliest art ever made. Burned sticks from the fire were used to draw animals onto these cave walls in France around 30,000 years ago!

What Will You Need?

Different types of charcoal are great for different kinds of art. It might be worth buying a set if you don't already have any charcoal. Sets often include white, brown, and black charcoal pencils, vine charcoal, a compressed charcoal block, and a blending stump.

Vine Charcoal

These long, thin charcoal sticks are made by burning sticks or vines. They smudge and erase easily, so they are great for making sketches but not good for drawing detail.

Compressed Charcoal

Compressed charcoal is shaped into a block or stick using gum or wax. Soft sticks make dark marks. Firm sticks make lighter marks.

Charcoal Pencils

Charcoal pencils contain compressed charcoal. They are useful for fine, detailed drawing. The wood surround helps keep hands clean.

Erasers

An eraser pencil or a **kneaded eraser** are both useful for erasing and drawing.

Blenders

A blending stump or cotton swab will **blend** detailed areas.

Paper

Paper with a rough **texture** holds charcoal best. Charcoal works great with colored paper, too.

rough texture paper

You will also need wet wipes, paper towels, a cloth, acrylic or watercolor paint, soft pastels or chalks, masking tape, scissors, a spray bottle, and 2% milk.

Charcoal Techniques

It is really easy to get started using charcoal. Just pick up a stick and start to draw! There are some special charcoal skills that are useful to learn, though. Try some of the techniques on these pages to really get the hang of how to use it.

Hatching

To shade in an area using charcoal, try drawing several lines close to each other. The crumbly charcoal edges will blend into each other, creating a *solid block of black*.

Blending

Create a smooth grade from dark to light by blending the charcoal.

Hatch a dark area using heavy pressure. Make a paler area next to it using light pressure.

Try blending the two areas. You can use your finger, a cloth, or a blending stump. The blending stump gives the smoothest blend.

Rubbing

Try doing a charcoal rubbing. Place a sheet of thin paper over a textured surface. We used a sheet of *bubble wrap*. Using the edge of a charcoal stick, rub over the paper using even pressure. The texture of the surface should show through as a pattern on your paper.

Master Class

Lifting Using an Eraser

You can draw on charcoal-covered paper using an eraser. Try this project and draw a pumpkin using an eraser. You will need some orange paper, a stick of charcoal, and a kneaded eraser or an eraser pencil.

1 Create a dark charcoal background using the hatching technique.

2 Knead your eraser to a point. Draw a basic pumpkin shape. Then draw around the eyes, nose, and mouth.

3 Add the fine detail using an eraser pencil. Leave some black for the grooves on the pumpkin.

Be a Charcoal Expert

Now that you have mastered some charcoal techniques, here are some simple tips and tricks to help you along your way.

▶ Keeping Your Eraser Clean

As you have seen, erasers are a great tool to draw with. They can also help clean up any charcoal dust, or tidy up messy edges. You need to keep your eraser clean, though. A dirty eraser may end up adding charcoal, instead of taking it away!

1

To clean a kneaded eraser, wipe away any **excess** dirt using a tissue. Then pull the dirty area away from the rest of the eraser.

2

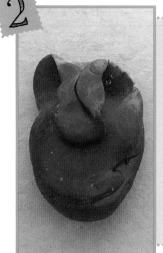

Now fold it into the center of the eraser. Knead the rest of the eraser around the dirty area. The eraser surface should now be clean.

TIP

To help keep your eraser clean in your pencil case, try this tip. Take two plastic bottle tops. Place the eraser in one lid and then press the second lid on top. Now you have an eraser carry case!

Charcoal Pencil Care

Charcoal is **fragile**, and this can be annoying if your pencil point keeps breaking. Sharpen your pencils using the large hole in a double pencil sharpener. Turn the sharpener, not the pencil. If the wood flakes off in small pieces, your blade may need replacing. You can also sharpen your pencils using coarse sandpaper.

Drawing with Dust

Is holding a stick of charcoal getting your hands too messy? Try scribbling a blob of charcoal onto a scrap of paper. Then dip a blending stump into the charcoal dust and draw with that instead.

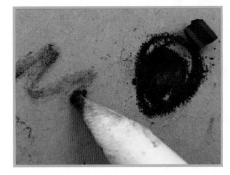

The Paper Trick

When your paper is covered in smudgy charcoal, it is hard to know where to rest your hand as you draw. Lay a piece of scrap paper over your drawing and lean on that instead.

Rub Away the Dark

Practice drawing squares of different **shades** using hard to soft pressure. To make the palest squares, dab away some of the charcoal using a cloth.

Using Stencils

A stencil is a sheet of card or plastic with holes cut into it. When you draw with charcoal over the card, it only marks the paper underneath in the places where the holes have been made. When you lift the card you can see the image. You could try using a stencil or making your own from cardboard. You could also try the simple project on page 11, and use your own hand as a stencil.

This ancient cave painting from Borneo, Indonesia, was done using people's hands as stencils.

TIP

When using a cutout stencil like this bicycle, try this technique. Tape the stencil to your paper. Scribble some charcoal on a separate piece of paper. Dip a scrunched-up tissue into the charcoal dust and then dab the charcoal over the holes of the stencil.

Master Class

Hand Stencil

Make your own cave art using your hand as a stencil. All you need is a stick of charcoal, some paper, and your hand. We used speckled drawing paper that looked a little like stone.

1

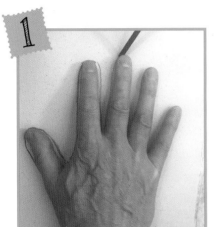

Draw around your hand using a stick of charcoal.

2

Draw a thick border around the edge of your outline using the side of the charcoal.

3

Blend the border outward using your finger.

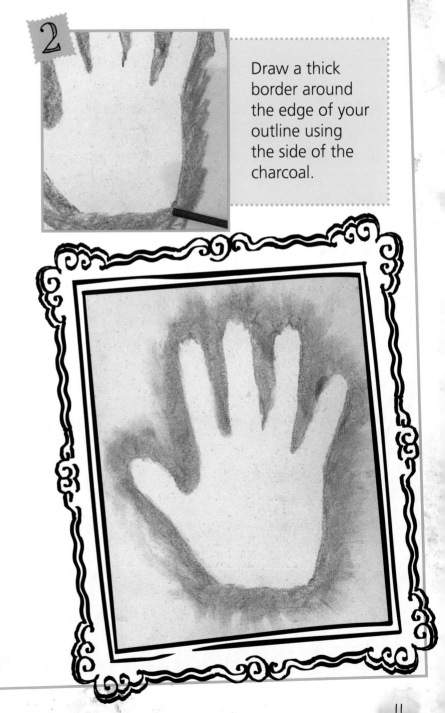

PROJECT PAGE:
Cave Painting

Use stencil and rubbing techniques to create this bear cave painting. You will need two sheets of paper or thin card stock, some masking tape, some tracing paper, a stick of charcoal, white pastel or white charcoal, and a cloth.

1

We used brown paper to make our picture look like it was drawn on a cave wall. Carefully tear around all the edges to make them **jagged**.

2

Lay your paper on some tree bark. Rub over the paper with a large stick of charcoal. The bark rubbing should create interesting uneven patterns on your paper.

3

Trace this bear outline onto tracing paper, then onto your other sheet of paper.

4

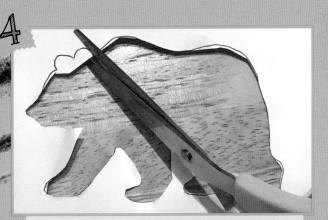

Carefully cut out your bear stencil. Poke your scissors into the center, and then cut around the body first. Leave the legs and ears until last. Ask an adult to help you.

5

Tape your bear stencil in place on the torn paper. Using the side of a large charcoal stick, gently rub over the stencil. It works best to rub upward when you do the bear's legs.

6

Remove the stencil but keep it safe for a project on page 15. You can outline your bear using a charcoal stick. Add a little white and black dot for the eye.

All About Fixative

As charcoal is so smudgy, you need a way to fix it to the paper when you are done with your picture. Artists use spray **fixative** for this. You can buy cans of fixative from an art store. Fixative can be expensive, and you must spray it outside. The chemicals in it have a very strong smell that can make you feel sick.

Some people use hairspray as fixative. It is cheaper, but does not work as well, and has a strong smell, too.

TIP

A great alternative to fixative is to use milk! Get an empty spray bottle. We used an old body spray bottle. Wash it out and put some 2% milk in it. When you want to fix a charcoal drawing, lightly mist the paper with the milk. Let it dry completely between coats. Three coats will usually fix the charcoal pretty well. Milk is great as it is cheap, easily available, and doesn't smell.

Try smudge-testing milk fixative. We drew three charcoal squares and dragged a finger across them after one spray and three sprays. Here are our results.

without fixative

after one spray

after three sprays

Master Class

Using Milk Fixative

Try this project using charcoal mixed with soft pastels or chalks. The milk helps fix the charcoal so it won't smudge when you add the color.

1

2

3

Tape your stencil onto a piece of textured paper. Fill in your bear using a charcoal stick.

Lift off the stencil. Add some grass, and fur on the bear. Spray your drawing, letting it dry between coats.

You should be able to use pastels or chalks next to the charcoal now, without much smudging.

Use red, orange, yellow, and white to create a sunset background. Blend the colors using your finger or a blending stump. Then spray with more fixative.

Make Abstract Art

Abstract art doesn't try to represent real things. Abstract artists use shapes, colors, and marks to create their art instead. The strong contrasts you get with charcoal look great in an abstract picture. Try one for yourself. You will need a pencil, charcoal stick, charcoal pencil, and a blending tool.

1

Using a pencil, draw some simple overlapping lines and shapes on your paper.

2

Using a vine charcoal stick, fill each area with a different shade or pattern.

3

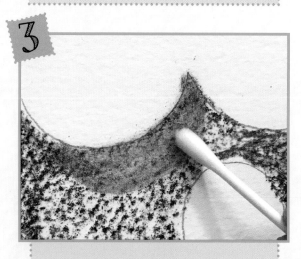

You can blend the charcoal using a cotton swab.

4

You can shade lighter areas such as these cloud shapes using the dirty cotton swab, too.

5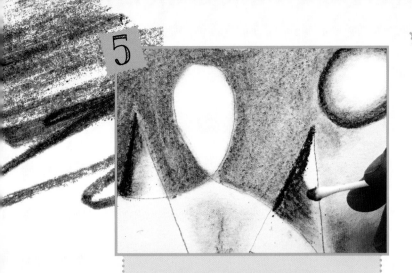

Try blending charcoal in some of the shapes from dark to light. Drag the color from one side using a cotton swab.

6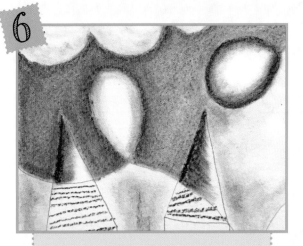

You could add stripes, checks, or spots to your shading, too.

When you have finished coloring in, you could go over your outlines using a charcoal pencil.

To create the balloon shapes, draw an outline of charcoal. Then gently blend the color toward the center.

Using Colored Paper

When you use charcoal on white paper, you can use the white of the paper as **highlights**. Colored paper can work really well with charcoal, too, if you select a suitable color for your picture. For example, in the eraser picture at the bottom of page 7, we used the orange of the paper to show through in places and give color to our pumpkin.

Selecting Your Color

Try picking a color that will match the subject of your drawing. For this leaf rubbing, we chose a green paper. The leaf rubbing then creates the leaves' outline and shadows.

TIP

To create a good leaf rubbing, choose leaves that have veins that stand out from the leaf. Use paper rather than card stock, so that you can feel the shape of the leaf through it as you rub. Use the side of a stick of compressed charcoal for the best result.

Master Class

Draw with an Eraser

Charcoal artists often color their paper with a layer of medium gray charcoal before they draw. They can then erase away any pale areas, and add any darker areas.

1

2

3

Apply a layer of charcoal onto some textured paper. Blend it using a cloth to color the whole paper a medium gray.

Knead your eraser to a point, or use an eraser pencil. Draw your design by erasing away the charcoal where you want any pale areas.

Now add any darker areas of charcoal. You can blend them using a cotton swab. We used **circular** strokes around our moon to make it appear to glow.

4

Add any really dark areas, such as outlines and trees, using a compressed charcoal pencil.

PROJECT PAGE:
Owl by Moonlight

You can create your own colored paper very easily by painting acrylic or watercolor paint onto watercolor paper. By creating your own colored paper, you can leave any areas unpainted that you want to keep white in your image.

1
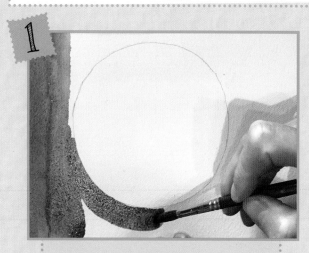

Draw a circle where you want your moon to go. Carefully paint around the circle using blue watercolor paint.

2

Once your paint is dry, add some texture to your moon using charcoal. You can smudge it around using your finger.

3

Add charcoal shading to each corner. Leave a blue circle around the moon, so it looks as if it is glowing.

TIP

If you use acrylic paint, add some water to it before you paint. If the paint is too thick, it fills the holes in your textured paper and the charcoal will have nothing to hold on to.

Draw your tree branch using a charcoal pencil. Overlap the bottom of the moon. That way, when your owl sits on a branch it will be near the center of the moon.

Add highlights to the tops of your branches using a white charcoal pencil or chalk. Sketch your owl in using a pencil.

Color your owl in using a charcoal pencil. Try to draw your lines in the direction that the feathers might grow.

Blending Practice

Can you make a flat circle look like a ball? Yes, with some simple charcoal shading, you can! Try this project and see for yourself.

1

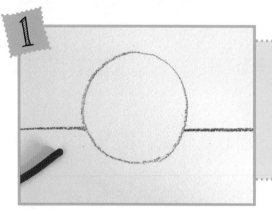

Draw a circle in the center of your paper using a charcoal stick. Draw a **horizon** line on each side. You can use a ruler to make sure each side is level.

2

Shade the background above the horizon line using a very dark charcoal. Blend the edges a little using a cloth.

3

Your light is coming from the left side, so leave a semicircle at the left of the circle unshaded. Draw a light charcoal **arc** using the lightest possible pressure next to the semicircle area you left blank.

4

Apply a little more pressure and draw another arc next to your first. Gradually apply more pressure as you move toward the edge, but leave a thin, unshaded arc at the very right hand edge. Light reflects off a pale surface and would light that area a little.

5

Blend your shading using a cotton swab or blending stump. If you move your hand in an arc as you blend, it will help make the circle look three-dimensional.

To finish your drawing, add a shadow on the table. Make the shadow dark near the circle and fade as it gets further away.

PROJECT PAGE:
Water Droplets

Now that you can shade a ball, try shading a water droplet. The liquid allows some light to enter it, rather than bounce off it. This means that you need to shade your water droplet shapes in a slightly different way than how you shaded the ball on pages 22 and 23.

1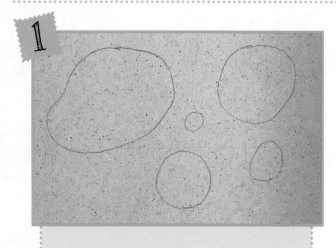

Draw some droplet shapes using a pencil. We used speckled gray paper, which will help any white highlights show up well.

2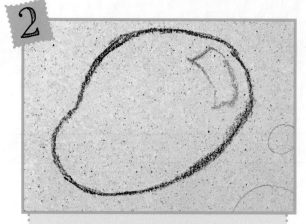

Outline your shape using a charcoal stick. Lightly outline a curved rectangle. This area will become a white highlight area.

3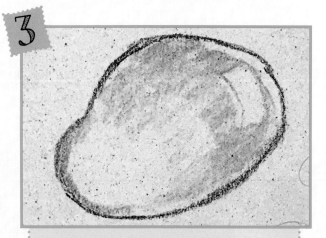

Lightly shade the right side of your droplet. Add a little shade to the far left edge, too.

TIP

Even though the water droplet's main highlight is on the right, the area around the highlight on a droplet is the darkest. Why? Light bends as it enters the droplet, making the largest pale area actually opposite the highlight side.

4

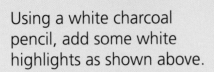

Using a white charcoal pencil, add some white highlights as shown above.

5

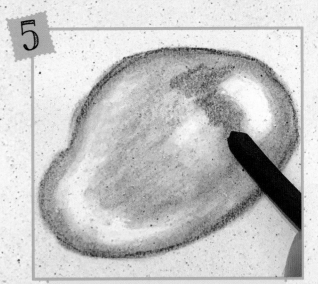

Add some darker shading around the main highlight on the right.

6

Add a dark charcoal outline around your droplet. Make the outline a little thicker on the highlight side. Smudge the edge a little with a cotton swab.

Add a few more droplets to your picture. Make them all slightly different sizes and shapes.

Using Lines

When we shaded the ball, you could see how the direction of the lines you made helped make the shape look **three-dimensional**. You can use different-shaped lines to give your picture other effects. Experiment with the thickness of your lines, too, by using the tip or the side of a charcoal stick.

Watery Lines

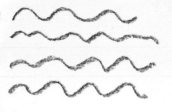

Try drawing wavy lines or circles using a charcoal stick.

When you blend the lines, they can help give the appearance of water.

TIP

Did you know you could paint with charcoal? Try dipping a small brush in water and blending your lines with the brush. You can mix charcoal dust with some water and paint using the mixture, too.

Master Class

Directional Lines

Try shading this pear using curved lines, highlights, and shading.

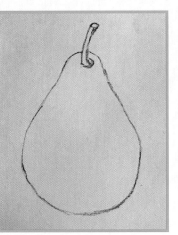

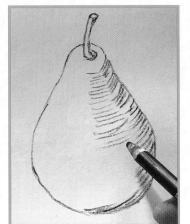

Draw a simple pear shape. You can trace this one if you like.

Add curved shading lines going around the pear.

Blend the lines using a blending stump or cotton swab.

Pick out any highlights using a kneaded eraser.

Add a horizon and a shadow under the pear.

Tornado

The direction of your charcoal lines can help add movement to your picture. Try drawing this swirling tornado using different hand movements and *see* how your lines really add drama.

1

Create a medium gray charcoal background, as you did for the eraser drawing on page 19. Using a charcoal stick, draw a horizon and a curving road. The road will get narrower in the distance.

2

To help the landscape seem to travel away from you, add some direction lines. With the side of a piece of charcoal, drag it along the paper following the curve of the road.

3

Add some dark, windswept trees and bushes along the horizon.

4

Using the point of a charcoal stick, draw the tornado's funnel.

5

Shade the left-hand side of the tornado's funnel using curved lines. Then blend the lines with a blending stick.

6

Holding a piece of charcoal flat, create the swirling cloud by moving your hand in a "U" shape above the funnel.

We added a fence, and some dust at the bottom of the funnel. The fence posts should get smaller as they get farther away.

29

Glossary

abstract Art using color, line, or texture with little or no attempt at creating a realistic picture.

arc A curved path.

blend To shade into each other.

circular Having the form of a circle.

excess An amount beyond what is needed.

fixative Something that fixes or sets.

fragile Easily broken or destroyed.

highlights The brightest spots or areas in a painting.

horizon The line where the Earth or sea seems to meet the sky.

jagged Having an uneven edge or surface.

kiln An oven or furnace for hardening, burning, or drying something.

kneaded eraser A moldable piece of rubber used to erase marks.

shade The darkness or lightness of a color.

sketching Creating a rough drawing representing the main features of an object or scene.

texture The structure, feel, and appearance of something.

three-dimensional Giving the appearance of depth.

vine A plant whose stem requires support and which climbs by tendrils or twining or creeps along the ground.

Further Information

Books

KidsArt. *Chalk and Charcoal*. Mt. Shasta, CA: KidsArt, 2018.

Pearce, Steven. *101 Textures in Graphite & Charcoal*. Lake Forest, CA: Walter Foster Publishing, 2018.

Websites

Children's book illustrator P. J. Lynch shows how he draws in charcoal:
www.theguardian.com/childrens-books-site/gallery/2016/jan/02/
   how-to-draw-with-charcoal-pj-lynch

Art For Kids video showing how to shade a sphere:
www.youtube.com/watch?v=tJT-CWpXh7Y&feature=youtu.be

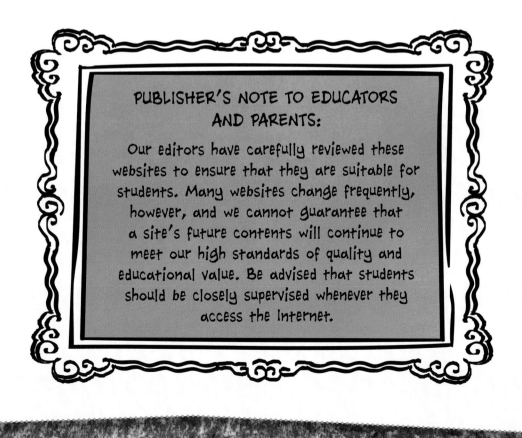

PUBLISHER'S NOTE TO EDUCATORS AND PARENTS:

Our editors have carefully reviewed these websites to ensure that they are suitable for students. Many websites change frequently, however, and we cannot guarantee that a site's future contents will continue to meet our high standards of quality and educational value. Be advised that students should be closely supervised whenever they access the Internet.

Index